THE COMPLETE
BRITISH SHORTHAIR CARE
HANDBOOK

Everything You Need To Know To Raise, Train, Feed, & Bond with Your Gentle British Shorthair Cat Pet

By

SYLAS THORNE

TABLE OF CONTENTS

INTRODUCTION 5

CHAPTER 1 12

OVERVIEW OF BRITISH SHORTHAIR TRAITS 12

Physical Characteristics: A Vision of Plush Perfection 12

Personality Traits and Temperament: A Perfect Blend of Independence and Affection 14

Comparing British Shorthairs with Other Breeds 16

Decoding British Shorthair Behaviors . 18

Socialization Patterns 21

Signs of Stress or Discomfort 23

CHAPTER 2 25

ESSENTIALS OF TRAINING BRITISH SHORTHAIR CATS 25

- Understanding Trainability in British Shorthairs 25
- Basic Training Techniques 26
- Advanced Training Skills 29
- Using Positive Reinforcement Effectively 31
- Common Challenges and How to Overcome Them 32

CHAPTER 3 33

CREATING THE PERFECT ENVIRONMENT 33

- Designing a Cat-Friendly Home 33
- The Importance of Routine 35
- Environmental Enrichment Ideas 37

CHAPTER 4 41

STRENGTHENING YOUR BOND 41

Building Trust with Your British Shorthair..................41

Quality Time Together..................44

Recognizing Your Cat's Unique Personality..................48

CHAPTER 5..................52

UNDERSTANDING HEALTH-RELATED BEHAVIOURS WITH BRITISH SHORTHAIRS..................52

Normal vs. Concerning Behaviours in British Shorthairs..................53

Recognizing Symptoms of Illness in British Shorthairs..................56

Common Health Issues in British Shorthairs..................58

Managing Aging and Mobility Issues....59

TROUBLESHOOTING AND FAQS..................64

THANKS FOR READING!!!..................71

INTRODUCTION

The Enchanting World of British Shorthair Cats

British Shorthair cats, with their plush coats, round faces, and iconic Cheshire cat-like smile, are among the most adored feline companions. Yet, beneath their captivating appearance lies a complex, charming personality that deserves deeper exploration. To truly appreciate and bond with these gentle, intelligent creatures, one must delve into understanding their unique behaviors. In this guide, we'll introduce you to the art and science of decoding British Shorthair behavior, explore why this understanding matters, and uncover the joys of bonding with this iconic breed.

Why Understanding British Shorthair Behavior Matters

Have you ever wondered why your British Shorthair seems to stare at you with those mesmerizing amber or blue eyes, only to walk away nonchalantly? Or why they seem to prefer lounging on your lap one day and a solitary perch the next? These enigmatic behaviors are more than quirks—they are your cat's way of communicating.

Understanding these behaviors isn't just about satisfying curiosity; it's a vital part of ensuring their happiness and well-being. British Shorthairs are known for their stoic nature, but this doesn't mean they lack emotions. Their subtle body language, vocal cues, and habits reveal how they feel and what they need.

When you can decode these signals, you become an active participant in their world, recognizing when they're stressed, playful, or content. This not only prevents potential behavioral issues but also strengthens the bond between you and your feline friend. It's the foundation of a relationship built on trust and mutual respect.

The Importance of Bonding with Your British Shorthair

Bonding with a British Shorthair is like cultivating a delicate and rewarding friendship. These cats are not as overtly needy as some other breeds; they won't demand constant attention or follow you around relentlessly. Instead, they are creatures of balance—reserved yet affectionate, independent yet deeply attached to their owners.

Why is this bond so important? For one, it enhances their quality of life. A cat that feels secure and loved will display fewer stress-related behaviors, such as excessive grooming or aggression. Moreover, a strong bond enables you to train your British Shorthair more effectively. While they are not as boisterously active as some breeds, they are highly intelligent and capable of learning commands, tricks, and even routines. The stronger your connection, the more eager they will be to engage with you.

But perhaps the most heartwarming reason to foster this bond is the joy it brings. There's something magical about a British Shorthair choosing to curl up next to you, trusting you with their relaxed, vulnerable self. These moments of connection remind us of the unique bond humans can share with animals—a relationship that transcends words.

The Personality of the British Shorthair: A Study in Elegance

To understand your British Shorthair's behavior, it's essential to first appreciate their personality. These cats are often described as the "gentle giants" of the feline world. They are sturdy and robust, not just in physique but also in character.

1. **Calm and Collected:** British Shorthairs are not prone to dramatic outbursts or erratic behavior. They exude a calm dignity, making them ideal companions for people seeking a low-maintenance but affectionate pet.

2. **Independent but Loving:** While they enjoy their alone time, British Shorthairs are deeply loyal. They may not always seek out your company, but they are quietly aware of your presence and enjoy being part of your household rhythm.

3. **Playful Yet Composed:** Don't mistake their calm demeanor for laziness. British Shorthairs enjoy interactive play, especially games that engage their hunting instincts. Feather wands, laser pointers, and puzzle toys are favorites. However, they tend to play with a sense of purpose, never devolving into wild, chaotic antics.

4. **Social but Selective:** These cats are friendly with strangers and tolerant of children and other pets, but they often form a special bond with one or two favorite humans. Winning their affection is a gradual process, but the loyalty they offer in return is steadfast.

5. **Inquisitive Thinkers:** British Shorthairs are observers. They will sit back and watch a situation unfold, processing it before deciding how to act. This reflective nature can make them seem aloof, but it's simply their way of understanding the world.

By embracing these traits, you'll start to see patterns in their behavior that are unique to them. You'll recognize their subtle signs of happiness, such as a slow blink or a gentle headbutt, and learn to respect their boundaries when they retreat to their favorite quiet spot.

Training & Decoding Behaviors: The British Shorthair Way

Training a British Shorthair isn't about imposing your will but rather understanding what motivates them. Positive reinforcement is key—these cats respond well to treats, praise, and affection. Patience is your best ally; their thoughtful nature means they may take time to grasp new concepts, but once they do, they rarely forget.

When decoding their behaviors, remember to observe their body language closely. A flicking tail or flattened ears may indicate discomfort, while a slow, deliberate tail wag often signals contentment. Their vocalizations are usually soft and infrequent, but pay attention to variations in tone—each sound carries meaning.

By dedicating time to understanding your British Shorthair, you'll unlock the secrets of their enigmatic world. This journey of discovery is one of the most rewarding aspects of sharing your life with this remarkable breed

CHAPTER 1
OVERVIEW OF BRITISH SHORTHAIR TRAITS

Physical Characteristics: A Vision of Plush Perfection

British Shorthairs are celebrated for their iconic, teddy bear-like appearance. Their compact, muscular build and dense coat set them apart from most other breeds. Here's a closer look at their defining traits:

1. **Build and Size**

   British Shorthairs are medium to large cats with a powerful, stocky physique. Males typically weigh between 9–17 pounds, while females are slightly smaller, ranging from 7–12 pounds. Their broad chests, thick necks, and strong legs contribute to their sturdy appearance.

2. **Head and Facial Features**

   One of the breed's most distinctive attributes is its round head adorned with chubby cheeks and a short, broad nose. The expressive eyes, often golden or copper, exude an aura of calm intelligence. Some British Shorthairs, particularly those with blue coats, may have mesmerizing deep amber eyes.

3. **Coat and Colors**

   The dense, plush coat of a British Shorthair is one of its hallmark features. The double-layered fur feels luxuriously soft to the touch. While the "British Blue" coat is the most iconic, this breed comes in an astonishing array of colors and patterns, including black, white, cream, tabby, and even bi-colored combinations.

4. **Tail and Ears**

   Their tails are thick and taper slightly towards the end, maintaining proportionality to their stocky frame. The ears are small and rounded, sitting wide apart, enhancing their teddy bear-like appearance.

Personality Traits and Temperament: A Perfect Blend of Independence and Affection

British Shorthairs are as endearing in character as they are in appearance. They embody a harmonious balance of independence and affection, making them adaptable companions for various lifestyles.

1. **Gentle and Calm Nature**

These cats are the epitome of tranquility. They seldom exhibit hyperactivity or destructive behavior, making them ideal for families, singles, or seniors looking for a peaceful pet.

2. **Affectionate Without Being Clingy**

    While British Shorthairs love their humans, they aren't overly needy. They're content to sit beside you rather than on your lap, and they prefer a quiet pat on the head to being held for long periods.

3. **Intelligent and Observant**

    Don't let their relaxed demeanor fool you—they are highly intelligent creatures. British Shorthairs are quick to learn routines and can even be trained to follow simple commands. They enjoy puzzle toys and interactive games that challenge their minds.

4. **Compatibility with Others**

This breed is wonderfully adaptable to households with other pets or children. Their unflappable demeanor means they rarely feel threatened and often coexist peacefully with dogs or more energetic cat breeds.

5. **Playful Yet Reserved**

   British Shorthairs enjoy playing, especially as kittens, but their energy levels taper off as they mature. Even in play, they maintain an air of dignity, often favoring a slow chase or a gentle paw swipe over frantic sprints.

Comparing British Shorthairs with Other Breeds

When compared to other popular cat breeds, the British Shorthair holds its own with a unique combination of traits. Here's how it stacks up:

1. **Vs. Maine Coons**

   While both breeds are known for their large size, Maine Coons are more boisterous and outgoing. British Shorthairs, on the other hand, are more reserved and dignified. Maine Coons have longer fur and a more rugged appearance compared to the plush short coat of the British Shorthair.

2. **Vs. Siamese Cats**

   Siamese cats are highly vocal and demand constant attention, whereas British Shorthairs are quieter and more independent. The sleek, slim build of a Siamese is the polar opposite of the British Shorthair's rounded, robust physique.

3. **Vs. Persian Cats**

   Persians share the British Shorthair's love for a calm environment, but their long fur requires significantly more grooming.

British Shorthairs are lower maintenance and generally more playful than their Persian counterparts.

4. **Vs. Ragdolls**

   Ragdolls are known for their ultra-affectionate, floppy nature, often seeking constant physical closeness with their owners. British Shorthairs, while loving, maintain their independence and are less inclined to demand lap time.

5. **Vs. Bengal Cats**

   The Bengal's high energy and wild appearance make it a stark contrast to the serene British Shorthair. While Bengals thrive on adventure and climbing, British Shorthairs are happiest lounging near their humans.

Decoding British Shorthair Behaviors

Common Behaviors and Their Meanings

1. The "Silent Observer" Stare

One of the most iconic behaviors of British Shorthairs is their contemplative stare. Unlike more vocal breeds, these cats often use their gaze as a primary communication tool. A direct, unblinking stare often signifies curiosity or attention, especially if they're watching you cook, type, or perform other activities. However, if their pupils are dilated and their body stiff, the stare may indicate unease or hyper-awareness.

2. Purring Variations

Purring isn't always a blanket sign of happiness. In British Shorthairs, a deep, steady purr typically reflects contentment, especially during petting or after meals. However, a more sporadic or high-pitched purr might indicate they're seeking comfort, particularly in stressful situations like vet visits or unfamiliar environments.

3. Tail Talk

Their thick, plush tails offer a wealth of information. A tail held upright with a slight curve at the tip signifies friendliness and openness. If the tail is puffed up and bushy, it's a classic signal of fear or defensive readiness. A slowly swishing tail can denote irritation, while rapid flicks often indicate overstimulation.

4. The "Chirp" or Trill

British Shorthairs are less vocal than many breeds, but they occasionally emit chirps or trills. These sounds are affectionate greetings, often directed at their favorite humans. If your British Shorthair chirps when you walk in the door, it's their way of saying, "Welcome home!"

5. Kneading Rituals

Kneading, where the cat presses its paws rhythmically into a soft surface, harks back to kittenhood. For British Shorthairs, it's a soothing behavior tied to comfort and trust. If they knead on your lap, consider it a high honor—they see you as a source of safety and warmth.

Socialization Patterns

1. A Reserved Yet Loyal Nature

British Shorthairs are often described as the "gentle giants" of the feline world. While they may not demand attention like more boisterous breeds, they form deep, enduring bonds with their families. They prefer calm, consistent interactions over noisy, chaotic environments.

2. Gradual Warm-Ups to New Faces

These cats aren't typically social butterflies; they approach strangers with caution. When introducing a British Shorthair to guests, give them time to observe from a distance before attempting direct interaction. Once they've assessed the situation, they may come forward for a brief sniff or rub, signaling their tentative approval.

3. Play Preferences

British Shorthairs have a playful streak, but their style is more methodical than frenetic. Interactive toys like feather wands or puzzle feeders tap into their hunting instincts without overwhelming their laid-back personalities.

4. Social Hierarchies with Other Pets

In multi-pet households, British Shorthairs tend to be peacekeepers. They avoid confrontations and often find quiet corners to observe the dynamics. However, early socialization is key to fostering harmonious relationships with other cats or dogs.

5. The Art of Independent Companionship

One of their most endearing traits is their balance of independence and affection. British Shorthairs enjoy your presence but don't demand constant attention. They're content to sit nearby as you work or read, offering quiet companionship without being intrusive.

Signs of Stress or Discomfort

1. Altered Eating or Grooming Habits

A sudden decrease in appetite or obsessive grooming can be a red flag. Overgrooming, especially in the same area, may indicate stress, allergies, or even skin conditions. On the flip side, neglecting grooming altogether could signal depression or physical discomfort.

2. Hiding Behavior

While British Shorthairs enjoy occasional solitude, excessive hiding is a sign something is amiss. If your cat is retreating to secluded spots for extended periods, it's worth checking for environmental stressors, such as loud noises or changes in routine.

3. Vocalizations of Distress

Although not overly vocal, a British Shorthair in distress may yowl, hiss, or growl. Pay attention to the context—these sounds often accompany fear, pain, or territorial disputes.

4. Unusual Aggression or Defensiveness

A normally calm British Shorthair that suddenly becomes aggressive may be experiencing stress or discomfort. Watch for signs like flattened ears, a swishing tail, or raised fur, and consider consulting a vet if the behavior persists.

5. Changes in Litter Box Habits

Inappropriate elimination, such as urinating outside the litter box, is often a sign of emotional or physical distress. Ensure the litter box is clean and accessible, and consider whether recent changes in the household might be causing anxiety.

CHAPTER 2
ESSENTIALS OF TRAINING BRITISH SHORTHAIR CATS

Understanding Trainability in British Shorthairs

The British Shorthair is known for being laid-back, affectionate, and intelligent. However, they are also independent thinkers who may not respond to training in the same way as a dog would. Understanding their trainability starts with appreciating their temperament:

- **Independent but Affectionate**: British Shorthairs value their independence but thrive on love and attention from their owners. They're more likely to engage in training when they feel secure and bonded to you.

- **Moderate Energy Levels**: While they're not as high-energy as some breeds, British Shorthairs still enjoy playtime and mental stimulation. This makes training sessions a great opportunity to engage their minds.
- **Curiosity**: Their natural curiosity can be leveraged in training. Activities that pique their interest or involve exploration will hold their attention longer.

Unlike dogs, cats often need to see a clear benefit to participating in training. British Shorthairs, with their intelligence, are no different. Understanding what motivates them—whether it's a tasty treat, a favorite toy, or simply your attention—is key.

Basic Training Techniques

Starting with the basics helps establish a foundation for more advanced skills later. Here are the essentials:

1. Setting Up for Success

- **Timing Matters**: Choose a time when your cat is relaxed but alert. Avoid training when they're tired, hungry, or overstimulated.

- **Short Sessions**: Cats have short attention spans, so keep sessions to five to ten minutes. It's better to have multiple short sessions than one long one.

- **Environment**: Train in a quiet, distraction-free space. Remove other pets or anything that might divert their focus.

2. Teaching Name Recognition

Teaching your British Shorthair to respond to their name is the foundation of training.

- Use a cheerful tone and say their name. When they look at you, reward them immediately with a treat or praise.

- Repeat this several times a day, gradually increasing the distance between you and your cat.

3. Litter Box Etiquette

British Shorthairs are naturally clean and usually take to litter training easily.

- Show them the location of their litter box, and ensure it's always clean.
- If accidents occur, never scold. Instead, clean thoroughly to remove odors and encourage them to use the box next time.

4. Sit Command

Training your cat to sit is both practical and impressive.

- Hold a treat slightly above your cat's head. As they look up, their bottom will naturally lower.
- As soon as they sit, say "Sit" and reward them.

- Repeat consistently, using the same verbal cue each time.

Advanced Training Skills

Once your British Shorthair has mastered the basics, you can move on to more advanced skills. These activities will not only impress but also provide much-needed mental stimulation for your cat.

1. High-Five or Shake Paw

- Hold a treat in your hand and wait for your cat to paw at it.
- When their paw touches your hand, say "High-Five" or "Shake," then reward them.
- With consistency, they'll associate the action with the command.

2. Leash Training

British Shorthairs can be trained to walk on a leash, allowing them to safely explore the outdoors.

- Start by introducing them to a harness. Let them sniff and play with it before attempting to put it on.
- Once they're comfortable wearing the harness indoors, attach a lightweight leash and let them drag it around.
- Gradually progress to walking them on the leash, using treats to guide and reward positive behavior.

3. Puzzle Solving

Engage their intelligence with puzzles. Hide treats in puzzle toys or under cups, and encourage them to find the reward.

Using Positive Reinforcement Effectively

Positive reinforcement is the cornerstone of successful training. British Shorthairs respond best to encouragement and rewards rather than punishment.

1. Identify Motivators

Determine what your cat values most. Treats like freeze-dried chicken or salmon are usually a hit, but some cats respond better to praise or play.

2. Timing is Everything

Reward behaviors immediately so your cat understands the connection between the action and the reward.

3. Avoid Punishment

Scolding or punishing a cat can damage trust and discourage them from engaging in future training sessions. Focus on redirecting unwanted behaviors instead.

4. Gradual Progression

Build on successes gradually. Once your cat has mastered one skill, challenge them with the next step.

Common Challenges and How to Overcome Them

Training British Shorthairs may not always go smoothly, but persistence and understanding will help you navigate any obstacles.

- **Disinterest**: If your cat seems uninterested, reevaluate the motivators or timing of your sessions.
- **Short Attention Spans**: Keep sessions brief and end on a positive note, even if progress is minimal.
- **Behavioral Hiccups**: If unwanted behaviors arise, address them calmly and consistently.

Training your British Shorthair is as much about strengthening your bond as it is about teaching them tricks or commands. With patience and positivity, you'll not only have a well-behaved feline but also a deeper connection with your furry friend.

CHAPTER 3
CREATING THE PERFECT ENVIRONMENT

Designing a Cat-Friendly Home

Creating a space that feels like a sanctuary for your British Shorthair requires understanding their specific preferences and behaviors. These cats are moderately active and love their independence, so your home should cater to their needs for exploration, comfort, and safety.

1. Cozy Retreats:

British Shorthairs value their privacy and enjoy having quiet spaces to retreat to. Invest in plush cat beds or covered igloo-style cat houses placed in low-traffic areas. Position these spots near windows or in corners, where they can bask in sunlight or enjoy a bird's-eye view of the world outside.

2. Vertical Exploration:

Although not avid climbers like some breeds, British Shorthairs enjoy moderate vertical exploration. Install sturdy cat shelves or a multi-tiered cat tree in a neutral area. These additions not only satisfy their curiosity but also offer exercise and a safe perch to survey their surroundings.

3. Scratch and Stretch:

A scratching post is essential for maintaining your cat's claw health and protecting your furniture. Opt for vertical and horizontal scratching options covered in sisal or jute, as these textures appeal to their natural instincts. Placing these strategically near sleeping areas can encourage use right after a nap.

4. Safe Play Zones:

British Shorthairs are playful but prefer structured activities over chaotic play. Dedicate a corner of your home to their toys, such as puzzle feeders, plush mice, or feather wands. Rotating these toys regularly keeps their interest piqued and prevents boredom.

5. Thoughtful Décor:

When decorating, choose materials that are both stylish and cat-friendly. Opt for easy-to-clean fabrics like microfiber or leather for furniture and secure breakables out of reach. Rugs with non-slip backings can help them navigate floors without sliding, ensuring safety.

The Importance of Routine

British Shorthair cats thrive on predictability. Their calm and composed nature is complemented by a structured daily routine that aligns with their needs and instincts.

1. Feeding Schedule:

Consistent meal times are crucial. Feed your cat at the same times every day to prevent anxiety and over-eating. Incorporate high-quality wet and dry food, tailored to their nutritional needs, and ensure fresh water is always available. Using a timed feeder can also help maintain regularity if you're away during the day.

2. Grooming Rituals:

Despite their short coats, British Shorthairs benefit from weekly grooming sessions to remove loose fur and promote bonding. Make it a calming experience by using soft brushes and rewarding them with treats. This routine keeps their coat shiny and minimizes shedding around your home.

3. Playtime Punctuality:

Setting aside specific times for interactive play ensures they get the stimulation and exercise they need. Whether it's a game of chase with a laser pointer or a slow, deliberate hunt with a fishing-rod toy, consistency in timing enhances their sense of stability.

4. Sleep Sanctuaries:

Respect their natural sleep-wake cycles by allowing them undisturbed rest during their downtime. British Shorthairs love their naps, and providing them with quiet, comfortable sleeping spots reinforces their sense of security.

Environmental Enrichment Ideas

Keeping a British Shorthair mentally and physically stimulated is as important as addressing their basic needs. Environmental enrichment taps into their instincts, encourages exploration, and strengthens your bond.

1. Interactive Toys:

Puzzle toys and treat-dispensing balls are fantastic for engaging your cat's problem-solving skills. These encourage them to work for rewards, stimulating their natural hunting instincts. Start with simple puzzles and gradually introduce more complex designs as they master each one.

2. Nature's Window:

British Shorthairs love observing the world outside. Enhance their viewing experience by placing cat perches or window hammocks near windows. Adding bird feeders or moving decorations outdoors can make their window-gazing sessions even more captivating.

3. DIY Adventure Zones:

Create a custom exploration area using cardboard boxes, tunnels, and ramps. These inexpensive setups offer endless fun, allowing them to climb, hide, and stalk prey-like toys. Incorporate scents like catnip or silvervine to heighten their sensory experience.

4. Sensory Play:

Stimulate their senses with diverse textures, sounds, and smells. Crinkly tunnels, jingling balls, and scent-filled sachets can captivate their attention. Rotate these sensory toys regularly to maintain novelty.

5. Companion Enrichment:

British Shorthairs bond deeply with their human companions. Spend quality time engaging in gentle grooming, cuddling, or simply sitting together. For homes with more than one cat, interactive toys designed for group play can encourage social bonding.

6. Safe Outdoor Time:

Consider leash training your British Shorthair for supervised outdoor adventures. Secure, enclosed patios or "catios" offer a safe way for them to experience nature while staying protected.

Creating the perfect environment for a British Shorthair is a rewarding journey. By designing a cat-friendly home, adhering to a consistent routine, and introducing enriching activities, you're setting the stage for a happy, healthy feline companion who feels cherished and secure.

CHAPTER 4

STRENGTHENING YOUR BOND

Strengthening your bond with a British Shorthair is an ongoing process that involves building trust, spending quality time together, and recognizing and embracing their unique personality traits. Here's a guide on how to do just that.

Building Trust with Your British Shorthair

Trust is the foundation of any relationship, and it's no different when it comes to your British Shorthair. Unlike some cats that are more social and outgoing, British Shorthairs are often more reserved and independent. It may take time to build trust with them, but once you do, you'll have a loyal companion by your side.

1. Patience is Key

British Shorthairs aren't typically the type of cats that will immediately warm up to strangers or even new environments. When you first bring a British Shorthair into your home, give them the space they need to adjust. Avoid forcing interaction or trying to pet them right away. Instead, let them explore their surroundings at their own pace. This allows them to feel more comfortable in their new environment without the pressure of constant attention.

2. Respect Their Boundaries

Cats are known for their love of personal space, and the British Shorthair is no exception. Respecting your cat's boundaries is crucial to building trust. If your British Shorthair is not in the mood for affection, don't force the issue. Over time, they will start to seek you out for affection when they feel comfortable. Look for signs that your cat is open to interaction, such as sitting near you or following you around the house.

3. Offer Positive Reinforcement

Building trust can be achieved through positive reinforcement. Use treats, praise, and gentle petting to reward good behavior and encourage your British Shorthair to engage with you. If they allow you to pet them, give them a treat or softly speak to them in a calm voice. This helps them associate your presence with positive experiences and can gradually increase their comfort level with you.

4. Be Consistent

Cats thrive on routine, and British Shorthairs are no different. Having a consistent routine in place will help your cat feel secure and comfortable. Whether it's feeding times, play sessions, or quiet time on the couch, consistency will help build a predictable environment in which your cat can trust you. They'll begin to learn that you are a reliable source of food, safety, and companionship.

Quality Time Together

While British Shorthairs are known for their independent nature, they still need quality time with their humans. These cats enjoy bonding moments that allow them to connect with you on a deeper level. The key is to find activities and moments that are mutually enjoyable and help strengthen the bond between you and your furry friend.

1. Playtime is Essential

Just because British Shorthairs are often independent doesn't mean they don't enjoy playtime. In fact, play is an important aspect of their daily routine. Engaging your cat in interactive play not only stimulates their mind but also provides an opportunity for bonding. British Shorthairs enjoy a good chase, so consider using toys like feather wands, laser pointers, or interactive puzzles that can keep them entertained while allowing you to participate in the fun.

Playtime is also a great way to express affection in a way your British Shorthair will appreciate. These cats are not overly cuddly but will often show their appreciation for quality playtime by following you around or sitting beside you after the activity. Remember, the goal is to engage them on their terms, and with patience, they'll begin to enjoy playtime with you more and more.

2. Quiet Moments of Connection

British Shorthairs are often described as "low-key" or "laid-back," and they are generally content to lounge around the house. One of the best ways to bond with your British Shorthair is by simply sharing quiet moments together. Whether it's watching TV on the couch, reading a book, or sitting near them while they nap, the presence of a trusted human is often enough to keep them content.

Consider sitting near your British Shorthair while they relax. You don't need to do anything special — just being nearby and offering calm companionship will help reinforce your connection. You might notice that your cat will gradually move closer to you, eventually curling up by your side or on your lap. These moments of quiet connection are essential for strengthening your bond with them.

3. Grooming Sessions

British Shorthairs are relatively low-maintenance when it comes to grooming, but they still benefit from regular brushing. Taking the time to groom your cat is not only beneficial for their coat but also provides a great opportunity to bond. British Shorthairs are usually tolerant of brushing, and it's a great way to show affection while helping them feel pampered. Use a gentle brush designed for short-haired cats and be mindful of your cat's comfort level during the process. If your British Shorthair enjoys grooming, they may even allow you to brush them for longer periods, which is a sign of their trust and affection.

4. Respecting Their Independence

Though it's important to spend quality time with your British Shorthair, it's equally important to respect their independent nature. British Shorthairs are not as clingy as some other breeds, and they may prefer their alone time. It's important not to take this personally. Instead, view it as a sign of trust and respect for their space. When your cat wants to be alone, provide them with a quiet, comfortable space to retreat to, such as a cozy bed or a favorite perch. They'll come to you when they are ready for attention, and in time, they will seek out your companionship more often.

Recognizing Your Cat's Unique Personality

Each British Shorthair has its own individual personality, and understanding these differences is key to strengthening your relationship. While many British Shorthairs share similar traits, such as a calm temperament and an independent streak, it's important to pay attention to the subtle differences that make your cat unique.

1. Observe Their Behavior

Take the time to observe your British Shorthair's behavior in different situations. Do they enjoy being petted in certain spots? Are they more active during specific times of the day? Do they like to perch on high surfaces, or do they prefer low, cozy spots? Understanding their preferences and tendencies will help you tailor your interactions to meet their needs and make them feel more comfortable around you.

For example, if your British Shorthair enjoys sitting in a certain spot by the window, join them there and talk to them softly. If they prefer solitude, respect their need for space, and they'll reward you with moments of affection when they feel comfortable.

2. Know Their Likes and Dislikes

Some British Shorthairs are more sociable, while others are more reserved. Some might love sitting on your lap, while others may prefer sitting beside you. By recognizing what your cat enjoys and what they don't, you can offer experiences they will find rewarding. Whether it's a favorite toy, a special type of food, or a preferred napping spot, catering to these preferences will help you strengthen your connection with your cat.

Likewise, it's equally important to understand your cat's dislikes. If they are not fond of being picked up, respect that boundary. If they seem to dislike certain types of petting or handling, adjust accordingly. Respecting their unique needs will help prevent misunderstandings and foster a stronger bond over time.

3. Encourage Positive Socialization

Though British Shorthairs are often more independent, it's still important to encourage positive socialization. If you have other pets or family members, allow your British Shorthair to interact with them at their own pace. The key to positive socialization is allowing your cat to feel in control of the situation. For example, if you have a dog in the house, allow your British Shorthair to observe the dog from a safe distance before allowing direct interaction. Similarly, when introducing new people, let your cat approach them on their own terms, avoiding forced introductions.

4. Recognize Their Affection Styles

Although British Shorthairs are not as outwardly affectionate as some other breeds, they still have their own ways of showing love. For example, they may follow you around the house, sit near you while you relax, or nudge your hand for attention. These subtle gestures are their way of saying "I trust you." Recognizing and responding to these forms of affection will help deepen your bond.

In some cases, your British Shorthair may even surprise you with more overt displays of affection, such as sitting on your lap, kneading you, or even purring loudly when you pet them. These are clear signs that they feel comfortable and secure in your presence.

CHAPTER 5

UNDERSTANDING HEALTH-RELATED BEHAVIOURS WITH BRITISH SHORTHAIRS

Understanding the health-related behaviours of your British Shorthair is crucial not only for maintaining their happiness but also for ensuring that they lead long, healthy lives. While this breed is generally sturdy and resilient, there are still various health concerns to be aware of, particularly as they age. By recognizing what's normal versus what's concerning, identifying symptoms of illness early, and understanding how to manage aging and mobility issues, you can be a responsible and informed pet owner, ensuring the wellbeing of your British Shorthair.

Normal vs. Concerning Behaviours in British Shorthairs

Understanding your British Shorthair's typical behaviour is key to noticing when something is amiss. These cats are usually calm, independent, and affectionate in their own way. However, it's important to be aware of the subtle differences between behaviours that are entirely normal and those that may indicate health problems.

Normal Behaviours

- **Affectionate but Independent**: British Shorthairs are known for their loyalty, but they don't typically demand constant attention. They enjoy being around their owners but can be just as content lounging alone. A healthy British Shorthair will happily greet you when you return home, but may also spend time quietly lounging in their favourite spot without seeming distressed.

- **Playful at Times**: While British Shorthairs are generally more laid-back than some other breeds, they do enjoy play sessions. They may engage in a burst of activity, chasing toys or interacting with you, but these moments are often short-lived. This breed isn't as hyperactive as others, and that's completely normal.

- **Healthy Grooming**: British Shorthairs have dense, plush coats that require regular grooming. While they may not be as obsessed with grooming as some other cats, they will still groom themselves adequately, and owners can help by brushing their coat a few times a week.

Concerning Behaviours

- **Excessive Hiding**: While British Shorthairs do enjoy solitude at times, if your cat suddenly becomes reclusive and hides for extended periods, it may be a sign of stress or illness. Cats tend to retreat when they're feeling unwell or anxious, so this could signal something wrong.

- **Change in Appetite or Drinking Habits**: A sudden loss of appetite or excessive drinking could point to a health issue. For example, an increased thirst and urination could be symptoms of diabetes, kidney disease, or hyperthyroidism, all of which are common concerns in older cats.

- **Lethargy or Difficulty Moving**: If your cat seems unusually tired, sluggish, or reluctant to move around, this could be a red flag. British Shorthairs are typically calm, but they shouldn't show extreme lethargy or difficulty in getting up or jumping onto furniture, especially when they've previously been active.

Recognizing Symptoms of Illness in British Shorthairs

Even though British Shorthairs are relatively healthy, like all cats, they can suffer from a variety of health conditions. It's crucial to spot symptoms early so that your vet can address potential issues before they worsen.

Signs of Illness to Watch For:

- **Changes in Litter Box Habits**: If your British Shorthair begins urinating outside the litter box, or if there's a noticeable change in the volume or consistency of their urine or stool, it could indicate an underlying issue. Diarrhea or constipation, for instance, may suggest gastrointestinal problems or even stress.

- **Weight Fluctuations**: Cats are naturally good at hiding weight loss, so a noticeable decrease in weight can often be a sign of a serious health concern. Conversely, unexplained weight gain might point to issues such as thyroid problems or an unhealthy diet.

- **Excessive Vomiting**: Occasional hairballs or vomiting after eating too quickly are relatively normal for British Shorthairs. However, frequent vomiting or vomiting accompanied by other symptoms such as lethargy, diarrhea, or loss of appetite could indicate a more serious issue such as kidney disease, gastrointestinal disorders, or infections.

- **Coughing or Sneezing**: While a bit of sneezing is common in cats, especially if they have allergies, persistent coughing or sneezing with nasal discharge may signal respiratory infections, asthma, or even more serious conditions like pneumonia.

- **Changes in Behavioural Patterns**: A sudden change in behaviour such as becoming unusually aggressive, withdrawn, or vocal may be due to pain, discomfort, or an illness. Cats tend to hide their pain, so these behavioural changes are often an indication that something is wrong.

Common Health Issues in British Shorthairs

British Shorthairs are prone to a few breed-specific health conditions that are important to monitor:

- **Hypertrophic Cardiomyopathy (HCM)**: This heart condition, which causes thickening of the heart muscle, is common in British Shorthairs. Symptoms can be subtle, including lethargy, loss of appetite, and difficulty breathing. Regular check-ups with the vet, including heart scans, are vital for early detection.

- **Obesity**: Due to their love of food and tendency to be less active, British Shorthairs are prone to obesity. Obesity can lead to other health problems, including diabetes, arthritis, and heart disease.
- **Kidney Disease**: Older British Shorthairs are at an increased risk for kidney problems. Symptoms may include weight loss, decreased appetite, excessive drinking and urination, and lethargy.

Managing Aging and Mobility Issues

As British Shorthairs age, they can experience a variety of age-related health concerns. One of the most noticeable issues in older cats is the decline in mobility. Understanding how to manage these changes is key to maintaining your cat's quality of life.

Common Aging Issues in British Shorthairs:

- **Arthritis**: Just like humans, cats can develop arthritis as they age. This is particularly common in British Shorthairs due to their large size and muscular build. You might notice your cat moving less, showing discomfort when jumping, or avoiding stairs or furniture.

- **Reduced Activity**: Aging cats tend to be less active. British Shorthairs, which were once known for their playful bursts, might now be content to lie down for longer periods. While this is normal, any noticeable loss of activity or difficulty in getting up should be addressed by a vet.

- **Vision and Hearing Loss**: Older cats may develop impaired vision or hearing, which can lead to changes in their behaviour. They may seem disoriented or have difficulty navigating their environment. Bright lighting and easily accessible places to rest can help older cats with these sensory impairments.
- **Cognitive Dysfunction**: Similar to humans, cats can develop cognitive dysfunction syndrome (CDS) as they age. This condition causes confusion, disorientation, and a decline in social interactions. If your cat seems to forget where they are or forget you, it may be an early sign of cognitive decline.

How to Help Your Aging British Shorthair

- **Joint Supplements**: If arthritis is affecting your cat, joint supplements such as glucosamine and chondroitin can help improve mobility and reduce pain. Consult your vet for the right dosage and formulation.

- **Soft Bedding and Easy Access**: Make your cat's life easier by providing soft, low bedding and ensuring that their favourite spots (such as the windowsill or bed) are easy to access. For example, if your British Shorthair is having trouble jumping, providing ramps or low-step stools can help.

- **Regular Vet Check-Ups**: As your cat ages, regular vet visits become even more important. Annual or bi-annual check-ups can help detect any potential health issues early, particularly those related to mobility, heart health, or kidney function.

- **Diet Adjustments**: Senior cats often need special diets that are easier to digest and provide the nutrients necessary for aging bones and muscles. Your vet may recommend a senior formula food that helps with joint health and weight management.

TROUBLESHOOTING AND FAQS

1. Why is my British Shorthair not responding to training?

British Shorthairs can be independent, and while they are intelligent, they may not be as eager to please as other breeds. Be patient, use positive reinforcement, and keep training sessions short and consistent to maintain their interest.

2. How can I stop my British Shorthair from scratching furniture?

Provide scratching posts and pads in different textures and locations. Reward your cat when they use these instead of the furniture. You can also use scratching deterrents like sprays on furniture to discourage the behaviour.

3. Why is my British Shorthair not socializing with guests?

British Shorthairs tend to be reserved and may take time to warm up to new people. Ensure that guests are calm, quiet, and allow the cat to approach them when it feels comfortable. Avoid forcing interaction.

4. My British Shorthair seems overweight. How do I get it to lose weight?

British Shorthairs are prone to weight gain due to their relaxed nature. Ensure they have a balanced diet with controlled portions and encourage regular playtime to keep them active.

5. Why does my British Shorthair purr all the time?

Purring in British Shorthairs is often a sign of contentment. However, excessive purring can indicate stress or discomfort, especially if it's accompanied by other behavioural changes. Monitor their health and environment for stressors.

6. How can I stop my British Shorthair from being so vocal?

If your British Shorthair is excessively vocal, it may be seeking attention or expressing boredom. Engage in regular playtime to tire them out and offer comfort and companionship when needed.

7. Why does my British Shorthair have sudden bursts of energy?

British Shorthairs can experience bursts of energy, often referred to as "zoomies." These are completely normal, especially if your cat has been resting for a while. Ensure they have toys and climbing structures to channel this energy.

8. How do I stop my British Shorthair from knocking things off counters?

British Shorthairs may knock objects off counters due to curiosity or boredom. Provide more stimulation through interactive toys and ensure their environment is enriched with climbing spaces and safe areas to explore.

9. Why does my British Shorthair get anxious around certain people or situations?

Anxiety in British Shorthairs can stem from a lack of socialization or previous negative experiences. Gradually desensitize your cat by introducing new situations or people slowly and providing reassurance.

10. How can I train my British Shorthair to use the litter box?

Most British Shorthairs instinctively use the litter box, but some may need encouragement. Ensure the litter box is clean and in a quiet, accessible location. If accidents occur, avoid punishment and gently guide them back to the box.

11. Why does my British Shorthair have a "resting grumpy face"?

The British Shorthair breed naturally has a round face with a serious expression. It's not a sign of mood or discomfort but rather the cat's physical features.

12. How do I stop my British Shorthair from biting?

Biting is often a sign of overstimulation or play aggression. Recognize the signs of overstimulation and stop interaction before it leads to biting. Redirect their attention to toys for proper play.

13. My British Shorthair seems to be ignoring me. Should I be concerned?

British Shorthairs are not as overtly affectionate as other breeds, but they still enjoy companionship. They may prefer quiet, low-key interactions. If they're eating, grooming, and using the litter box normally, they're likely not distressed.

14. How do I keep my British Shorthair entertained?

Interactive toys, puzzle feeders, and cat trees can keep a British Shorthair mentally and physically stimulated. Regular playtime is key to prevent boredom and associated behavioural issues.

15. Why does my British Shorthair follow me everywhere?

This behaviour is a sign of attachment and trust. While British Shorthairs can be independent, they often enjoy being near their owners for comfort and reassurance.

16. Why does my British Shorthair act aloof?

British Shorthairs are often reserved but affectionate on their terms. Their aloofness is a natural trait, and they may prefer to observe rather than engage actively, unlike more extroverted breeds.

17. How can I train my British Shorthair to stop jumping on counters?

Consistency is key. Use positive reinforcement when they stay off counters, and provide alternative high spots like cat trees. Use deterrents like double-sided tape or aluminum foil to discourage the behaviour on counters.

18. What can I do if my British Shorthair is territorial?

British Shorthairs can be territorial, especially with other pets. To manage this, provide separate spaces for each pet and gradually introduce them to each other. Make sure resources like food bowls, litter boxes, and resting spots are separate.

19. How do I know if my British Shorthair is in pain?

Signs of pain in British Shorthairs include changes in grooming habits, refusal to eat, and avoidance of activity. If you suspect your cat is in pain, it's best to consult with a veterinarian.

20. My British Shorthair is licking excessively. What should I do?

Excessive licking could indicate stress, skin irritation, or health issues. Monitor your cat's behaviour, and if it continues, consult your veterinarian to rule out underlying problems.

THANKS FOR READING!!!

Printed in Dunstable, United Kingdom

75778224R00040